Riding the Waves of Thought:
Coping with Adversity through Poetry

By Jason Roger Pache

Thoughts come at us like waves in the ocean - both terrifying and exhilarating. We can ride the waves of thought through learning how to surf these waves. One way to surf with these waves is through fully immersing our mind in reading and writing in literature and philosophy – like fully immersing our body when we bodysurf a wave. And like bodysurfing in a wave, literature and philosophy can allow us to immerse our soul into the ocean-soul of being, lifting us to new heights, catching us as we go over the falls, and sustaining us as we glide across the ocean's glassy surface. Like the need for appreciating beauty, a meaningful life depends on discovering a way to glide over the ocean of thought and, to a fulfilling life, finding a way to flow within these undulations is indispensable to finding inspiration. However, like the bodysurfer left without a means to catch a wave if he or she is without fins on his or her feet, we find ourselves in this same predicament when we are without words to help us appreciate the beauty of the spiritual and intellectual movements that are carried by waves of thought. In this book, you will find the vocabulary of literature and philosophy in which you will discover ways of coping with adversity – the crash of waves in front of you – to let you plunge under the redoubtable terror of their prodigious immensity, until you arrive beyond the breakers, ready to catch the next wave onto the heights of poetic ecstasy. The enjoyment of the literary arts and philosophical speculation, like bodysurfing waves, is a lifelong and rapturous pursuit, and, once you start, you cannot stop enjoying the union of your soul with the ocean-soul of being that is the essence this soulful enrapture. Herein is an offering of vocabulary enhancement that will acquaint you with the beauty of the written word. These words speak in the language of literature and philosophy and are like the fins of a bodysurfer offering a means of being buoyed by – and flowing within – the soulful undulations of the ocean of thought.

Putting yourself to the test
And then following it with a period of rest
Will keep you operating at your best

Finding a place to dwell
Will keep your being well

Learning to endure
Will help you feel secure

Meaning restores you
Without needing to force you

It's best to not use force
But let time run its course
Because using force
Will only make things worse

You can be a part of love's efflorescence
When you are in the divine presence
Contemplating the essence
Of love's lessons

You can find a place where you can sit and dwell
And find out what your conscience has to tell

That for which you should have pride
Consists in a will to confide

To be friendly
Let others' judgments be

You can gain insight
By trying not to incite

The best mission
Of the human condition
Is to learn how to listen

Rules devised
Should periodically be revised

Meaning you can always make
No one from you can that gift take

You can procure a cure
From the will to endure

If you're moved to act
Try to do so with tact

The will to submit will help you to, your anger, quit.
And, with less anger, you're in less danger to, a mortal sin, commit

The will to confide
Will help wounded pride

To resist temptation
Deserves commendation

The duration
Of frustration
Will equate with an equivalent elation

The ultimate desideratum
Is to recover when you hit bottom

Honesty will promise thee
A solution eventually

You will be pure
If you can learn to inure

Learning to inure
Is a process of learning to endure

If life seems unfair
Just remember that you have always been able to repair

You know you're doing alright
If you can do what's right
Without needing to fight

Let love define
That which you keep in mind

To exude auspiciousness
Is to grant spontaneous wishes

Generosity will instill
A good will

To find a way to hope
Bring love within your scope

Let diversity
Be your university

Sometimes letting yourself drift
Can give you a lift

To find comfort in a thought
Means that you have found what you have sought

Learning to deliberate
Can be the solution for thoughts that tend to perseverate

Gestation
Born of Frustration
Bears Elation

It's alright
Not to fight

Coming to accept your fate
Will help to let your anger abate

You can be a non-conformist
In order to be a moral reformist

You can do what's right
Without having to fight

Who knows what the future will show
It's best just to let it go

Let time take its course
To lessen remorse

A solution will always arise
Once your will, with patience, complies

Let your pride
Reside
In practicing to habitually elide
Instances of wanting to deride

Integrity
Depends on
Sincerity

To be willing to digress
Sometimes helps you to progress

To inure yourself to pain
To a degree
As much as can be
Is to make a gain
That will eventually set you free

To restrain your greed
Let virtue intercede

Feeling contrite
Will help you do what's right

If you seek to work iniquity
Your enemies will be in ubiquity

Tradition
Can help with prediction
And to act with conviction
As a benediction
Of the human condition

Meaning always emerges
And converts to virtue what virtue urges

When you're at the stage
Of the sage
Never do you enrage

It will let agitation abate
If, though you may not approve, you still accept,
Your fate

You can figure out
How you can contribute
And make goodwill
A helping attribute

When you learn how to let your being settle
You learn how to put yourself in fine fettle

To abstain
From inflicting pain
Will help you retain
Your good name

It's better to repent
Than resent

It's best to confide
If you can't keep it inside

You need not feel non-plussed
At another's disgust
Because you need not feel you must
In all cases trust
That is one way to be wise
With which a good nature complies

Life is an ongoing process
In which you learn from your losses

You can give yourself dignity
Through benignity

Rules that get enforced
Provide an incentive
To keep your life on course
And be, umbrage, preventive

You're at home
When you've witnessed a gnome

To make the sacrifice of not eating animals
Will help one concentrate on the intangibles

You may get results
By being unkind
But that will mess
With your peace of mind

A prudent measure
Of pleasure
Will let you still retain
Heaven's treasure

When I cause
Others pain I, to myself,
Do the same

The notion
Of the ocean
Will help you cease commotion

You need not be attached to things
The mind is sufficient for what joy brings

You'll have fewer needs in life
If you can learn to endure strife

To endure will build your tolerance
Use restraint to get yourself hence

Gnostic knowledge derives from epiphanies
But long-suffering is more of what guarantees

A fondness for others happens in time
It leaves you with a love sublime

A fortuitous convergence of events
Will at times get you hence

You will worry less
If you can be in a hurry less

Noise
Is in-
Escapable
It's best to put up with it
As much
As you are capable

Enthusiasm is good
So long as it keeps you on the side of the good

Ignominy
Is saved
By bonhomie

A higher
Desire
Seeks to retire
From desire

The thought that you will encounter a meaningful trope
Will help to keep up hope

Sometimes to digress
Is to progress

Learning to endure
Will help you feel secure

A good deed
Will help a person in need

To regain
(Of mind) a healthy frame
Once the pain
Of shame
Has ceased to blame
And the brain
Gets back to feeling sane
Again

The practice of humility
Cultivates patience, which is an ability

When, concerning the truth
Let us speak it with ruth

So that love may endure to the end
Let peace and joy be a blend

Let anger abate
By having the patience to wait

When you encounter a trope
On the subject of hope
It can expand the scope
Of hope
And help you to cope

The proper counter conditioning of anger
Is the languor you feel later

You can learn a new trait
Each time you visit, of mind, a new state

Just because you're treated
Disrespectfully
Does not necessarily mean
That they see more than you see

The imagination can form a new reality
One approximating congeniality

You can learn to endure
Until you find the cure
To keep you pure

A flotation device
A buffer from being nice
Will help you be buoyant beyond vice

It's never trite
To do what's right

To submit to the moment
Helps you not to foment

Stop before you get angry
So you can know
That you can let
The anger go

You can learn to endure
What you cannot cure

Some people like to make others feel pain
And then make them feel shame
As though they were to blame
For their pain

The progression
Of aggression
Is into
Depression

Let the soul
Set its goal
In playing a role
In assimilating to good into the whole

Learning to endure
Can be as good as a cure
Because it helps you to inure

There is always a cause for concern
But that is how we learn

Learning to stop and be still
Will help you have goodwill

You know you've seen virtue defined
When its effect is salubrious to the mind

Contemplation helps you when you're sad
It helps you to refrain from getting mad
And gives your a reason for being glad

Phenomenology increases with your personal chronology
It manifests in the trajectory of your personal psychology

To not worry about where you fit in
Authenticity is a good place to begin

Some people are vindictive
But if you take umbrage your being will be constricted

Learn to let go when you start to fight
This will help you keep goodness in sight

The practice of enduring pain
Will help you to stay sane

It will help you in your prosperity
If you take into account the good of posterity

The eternal verities are what to cherish
Their meaning for your life will never perish

The world may seem cruel and demeaning
It's ok, you still can make meaning

To be free of the need to obfuscate
Will help you not to get irate

You can exercise your tolerance capacity
You'll be less offended at other's audacity

When the world is portentous
And the phenomena momentous
Try not to put up your defenses
So as to be less contentious

If you feel that suffering
Has shriven you
You know that divinity
Has forgiven you

There's always a way you can find relief
You can do so once you've processed grief

Some people, though they don't know you, still discriminate
That's ok, when you're depressed, you can always regenerate

To declare the need to bamboozle
It would be better to give a book a perusal

You need not mind suffering
If it gives you a buffering

As evidence that we should not eat cows
How many people would work in a slaughterhouse?

A conviction
Of dereliction
Will hopefully give one a predilection
For a conviction
Away from dereliction

To hear sound
And still have a ground
Will, to your mental health, redound

A personality
Can offer congeniality
If it stays in a balanced reality

To learn
From what you discern
From needing to repeatedly return
To that which, for you, is of concern
Is to earn
What you learn

It's not a spiel
To say your pain is a big deal
If your pain is real

It does not matter how you fashion it
So long as it's compassionate

If you obsess less
You will be under duress less

To switch to a new goal
When the gestalt of the soul
Halts before it fulfills its role

Go with what you're feeling
When your senses are reeling
So long as that feeling
Does not compel anything
Against healing

To comport yourself with dignity
Base it on benignity

It helps when in sorrow
To know there is tomorrow

It does not matter if something is trite
So long as it gives you an insight

To take care of your physical self
With help you have mental health

You can find delight
In doing what's right
So long as that right
Makes room for insight

To let your soul
Have its say
Will help your heart
Find a way

To live a life that's mindful
Is to live a life insightful

It helps to hold onto hope
And keep its objects in scope

To be sad
Rather than mad
Means it won't be that bad
To get back to glad

Let go into the moment
So as not to foment

Let continence play a role
In giving you self-control

The secret to peace of mind
Is to leave incontinence behind

No need to mind if your soul is feeling somber
If it helps you find peace because it helps you ponder

To not be attached to what you've got
Will save your from worrying a lot

The more your mind visits a mental state
The more it becomes a character trait

Learning not to indict
Will help you not to fight

To be a saint means to not be self-righteous
It means you solemnly try to indict less

You can find meaning in whatever you do
You can determine how you will construe

To wish to be transparent
Of one's flaws
Because they may only have an apparent
Cause
Having no factuality
Only an apparent actuality

You can know that you can be an angel now
Through trial and error you'll get there somehow

It's better to withstand
Than to command

No need to mind sacrificing time
To help someone who is in a bind

You can feel secure
When you think of all the times you've been able to endure

The will
To perform
Can make you an aggressor
It's best
To reform
And become a peace-professor

To not indulge
In exultation
Will teach you
Not to be attached
To your elation

Surrender unto the moment
When you start to get judgmental
To teach you not to foment
And not to be resentful

The less you let yourself fight
The more you'll experience insight

To know what to resist
And in what to persist
Is of what your mental health will consist

It will help you to allay worry
By not being in a hurry

The key to contentment
Is to lay to rest resentment

You can submit until the will is under control
To do this, it helps to turn attention to the soul

Healthy thoughts produce life-affirmations
They are contemplation's consecrations

Saints do what they can to help society
Without succumbing to the anger of contrariety

You can have your life depend less
On externals for success

Inspiration informs intuition
Aspiration sets you on a mission
If you can be calm
And live by the psalm
You can help your spiritual condition

Intuition tells you what to choose
Conscience tells you what to refuse

Education ensues
Upon resolution of the blues

Fellow-feeling is causative
Of the positive

You can learn to let go
To let yourself grow

From selfishness, you can achieve transcendence
If you can declare your independence
Without forsaking your descendants

To judge by intention
And not by effect
So long as effect
Teaches intention

To practice sublimation
Is to create insulation

You can let yourself be contrite
So that next time you'll do what's right

Observing the phenomena of the mind
Will help you to unwind

Learning to let resentments go
Will let forgiveness show

In our country, we have, with minorities, patience
That is what ranks us among the greatest of nations

The creation of cordiality
Can create a new reality

To renew an old meaning
In a new form
Is to imbue new feeling
Into that form

You can learn to prostrate
Rather than berate
And create
A fate
Less inclined to hate
And gravitate
To what is great
And learn to appreciate
The blank slate
For what it can create

You can learn to deliberate
To ease times when you start to perseverate

You can still
The will
To instill
Goodwill

Let the positive
Be your touchstone
To the truth
You call home

You can learn to dwell
So your feelings won't compel

To discover
How to hover
Is to live a life of love
Without co-dependence on a lover

Organic mental illness
Finds reprieve in stillness

You can learn to like
Without needing the other to requite

You can let the mind
Resign
And feel fine
In time

Let the soul
Console

Let rapid oscillation
Be your consolation

Rapturous contemplation
Brings rejuvenation

A trance will delight
When one loses one's might

Endurance
As a trait
Helps you
Accept your fate

Agitation
From too much cogitation
Finds its cure in vegetation

The presentation
Of contemplation
Brings condensation

One repents
To condense

You can learn to be still
And let the soul fill

You can put things in order
To make your next effort shorter

You can learn to consent
And not resent
When others dissent

A novel approach
Descends
When from self-reproach
You make amends

Learning to discriminate
Cause and effect
Will help you know
What you introject

Let intuition
Provide the source
Of a return to goodness
In due course

You can learn to be content
Once your opportunity's been spent

You can let the mind drift
To heal a rift
And let the spirit discern
How to return

You can have as one of your talents
The ability to stay in balance

You can let the self indulge
In learning to self-divulge

You can learn to sustain
Remaining the same
In the face of disdain

To subsist
Consists
In knowing when to resist
And when to desist

To be beholden
To the rule that is golden

To desist
Rather than to resist
Is in what sanity will consist

To practice sobriety
Can help to alleviate anxiety

You can turn the brood-words
Into good words

The articulate need to describe
The positive vibe

The compassionate relinquish
The need to extinguish

You learn not to gloat
When you realize we are all in the same boat

Let intuition
Render you a happy condition

You can revise
Where the truth lies
After you see things
Through another's eyes

You can retire from the race
And go at your own pace

To find redemption
In divine intervention
Gives one exemption
Wherein one is exempt
Form self-contempt

You've made progress
When you worry less
That to digress
Is to regress

To rein it in
So as to begin again

To not need to bluster
When you feel a fluster

If you want your lust to diminish
Get fast as you can from start to finish
Without needing to gratify
In order to satisfy
So that your chastity may be pure without a blemish

You can ease vertigo
By learning to take it slow

You can learn to dwell
Until you feel well

Being nice
Gives you a reward that's twice

Though you may feel you write drivel
It expresses feelings
And can make you civil
In future dealings

It helps you to cope
When you expand the scope
Of all that gives you hope

It helps to float
So as not to gloat

Time will tell
Which values work well

To be able
To take back in the self
That which you
Put on a shelf

To not base the meritorious
On whether it will make you glorious

You can make it your creed
To eschew greed

To commit to truth
So long as the truth you commit to has ruth

To be resigned
When the punishment is condign

To seek approximations in the will to perfect
The will to have on others a good effect

To keep pleasure pleasant
Take moderate measure in the present

Things could seem less drastic
If you remember it could all be stochastic

To dilate
Is to be less irate

Practicing forgiveness means:
At times you forgo the right
To indict
Over a slight

Happiness depends
On means as well as ends

To be thankful
For the dove
To overcome rankle
With love

Time can conduce
To the calling of a truce

To desire
To rewire
When you start to conspire

Let softness settle
So that soon you'll be feeling in fine fettle

To be great
Learn to let anger abate

Books plant seeds
That come to full flower in deeds

Trying not to gloat
(Because we are all in the same boat)
Will help you stay afloat

You can let your feeling flower
Impervious to power

You can distill
The thoughts that instill
Goodwill

Healing will occur
Each moment
That you defer
Not to foment

When you find
You are at the grind
Use your mind-
Fullness skill
To reorient the will

The willingness to compromise
Will help to keep you wise

To renounce
The will to denounce

In the ethic of care
The goal is to be fair

God puts you to the test
Jesus lays it to rest
He says you did your best

The Buddha
Went into the world
And learned tolerance
Enlightenment,
And compassion,
Was the consequence

Gaining a buffer
From when you suffer
Can provide insulation
For consolation

Sobriety
Helps society

You can know you have recourse
To letting time take its course

With the balm of understanding
You're no longer in need of reprimanding

To reduce
The need to induce
Can help produce
A truce

Its better not to use force
But instead let thoughts run their course

To be a friend to the self
As you would to someone else

You can take some time to dwell
So that your spirit may be well

To not mind taking oneself in the direction
Of perfection
So long as that perfection
Is amenable to correction

It's nice, of course, to be verbally fluent
But only if you're morally congruent

Some women
Are so quick
They must be an angel
To have such wit

You can self-train
To accept disdain
In order to stay sane

You can accept fate
To ease your state

To not worry so much about what you can do
As much as what you can, in contemplation, view

To be calm
In the crucible
Can be the fulcrum
Of what's useable

To learn
Not to be
Psyched out
Will help
Relieve you
Of doubt

Trying to be ok with pain
Will help keep you sane

To accept the fate that does befall you
Will help it not to gall you

You can soften pride
By learning to confide

Learning to stay calm
Will accustom you to the balm

You can importune
The bloom
To dispel the gloom

To settle your state
Try not to debate
Your fate

To try to find a positive explanation
For the different aspects of creation
Will give you a sensation
Of appreciation

You regain your equanimity
Once you practice benignity

If you recognize that life is on loan
Impermanence can then still be your home

Not to goad and spur
But to let thoughts occur

The goal
Is self-control
In a way
That is still good for your soul

You can curtail
The will to prevail

Regeneration
Through cooperation

To praise benignity
As the source of your dignity

Letting go of hate
Will help let your anger abate

The notion
Of the ocean
Can be like a healing potion

Let feeling guide
You away from that which would deride

To take a breath
And avoid the death
Of the moment you find yourself in
Inspiration will heal
The pain that you feel
And let the next creation begin

You can call it a loss
And forget about the opportunity cost

To give
Yourself a day
Of pleasure
So long as taken
In moderate
Measure
Will let you still
Partake
Of heaven's treasure

To give up
The need
To perform
Will give your happiness
A contemplative
Form

To give up the fight
So as not to indict

If you can withdraw into a cocoon
You will find a resolution soon

To the now
Try and submit
So that later
You will not commit
That which would later
Need to be remit

You need not mind
If others can read your mind
Because your will is kind

Another may not pay attention
But that doesn't mean they didn't give an inward mention

To be able
To live
With some compunction,
Although it's not ideal
It will help you
To function

Learning to dwell
Will help you more than you immediately can tell

Rejuvenation
Can come as a result
Of rumination

To be
Responsible
For one's behavior
And not let
Other's sadism
Turn into your anger

You can let go of hate
To let your anger abate

Those who are,
With their mockery,
Conformists
Will need to be
Later in life
Self-reformists

The fallacious
Of the salacious
Is that it is contagious
Of the umbrageous

You can lessen anxiety
By not practicing contrariety

Matching sound with sense
Will help to get you hence

You know you'll be ok
Even if you are pushed away
Because you have a mental place to stay

No apprehension of a motive is indubitable
Because it is inscrutable
And so, to it, what is attributable
Is disputable

You need not mind if another calls you "Fool!"
A fool can still obey the golden rule

Another may attempt to disturb you
But you don't have to let that perturb you

Writing thoughts helps you get relief
Writing helps you deal with grief
It helps you recall
That you recover every time you fall
So that the sway of despair will then be brief

Writing down your thoughts can bring you peace
And let your anguish go in soul-release
It teaches you how to deal
With the anguish that you feel
And helps you find your suffering surcease

A distillation
Of cerebration
Can give you a sensation
Of insulation

You can be glad you don't have to conform
And can obey your own norm

Some people look for ways to attack
Other people look for ways to hold back

Taking time to let your being expand
Will enable you to withstand
The reprimand

To endure
Censure
Can be an adventure
By which you mature

To be on public display
Without dismay

To be able
To relax
Without friends
Means that this limitation
Your happiness
Transcends

To dwell
Until the dream
Envelops
Is how
Creativity
Develops

The trick is to do what's right
But leave off before you fight

You can ride the intuition
To its fruition
Until analysis gives
Commission

Learning to compromise
Will help to keep you wise

To desire
To retire
From the will to conspire

To be improvident
Is to ignore the consequent

You can be open to all things
And see what joy brings

When others laugh
You can learn to stand the gaffe

If you can endure the dour of each day
This will help keep melancholy away

It's hard to know what other people think
Because perception alters in a blink

You're learning it's okay
To hesitate
Even though you may be late
Into society to integrate
It may be just your fate
That good things come to those who wait

It is sad that humans treat
Some animals as though they are just meat

If you experience anguish
From prolonged periods in which you languish
You're experiencing languish anguish

You can relieve your angst
When you find something for which to give thanks

You can find comfort in telling the truth
Because truth can be told with ruth

Thoughts will eventually run their course
You can be happy without using force

You can learn to tolerate energy
So as to benefit from a synergy

Doing without the need for clout
Can help you have less need to shout

Let intuition guide your way
And sanction what you say

To be real
Means not to conceal
How you feel

In your thoughts you can go deep-diving
For the sake of anagogic striving

To keep yourself from becoming a curmudgeon
It helps to forgo high dudgeon

You know you've experienced spiritual growth
If you can do without swearing an oath

If you can endure suffering with patience
You'll be less in need of seeking sensations

Virtue is known by the hope it breeds
Knowing this, you'll follow where virtue leads

It sets you on the spiritual path
When you forswear the use of wrath

Life
Is not
A contest
When
On principle
You're honest

That which you gain
Through nefarious skill
Will eventually undermine
The base of your goodwill

You will get
Your daily
Just desert
Each time
You resolve
Your inward hurt

It's better to yield
Than to wield

It's ok
To develop
Your talents
As long
As you stay
In balance

Let your conscience
Be
Your guide
And your intuition
Teach you what
To decide

The virtuously plausible
Is causable
So long as the cause
Gives a virtuous pause

Accepting that
From time to time
Your "reputation has been disvalued in levity" – Shakespeare, <u>Measure for Measure</u>
Will give you
A reputation of value
With longevity

In order to withstand pain
Acceptance eases the strain

The use of deceit
Ends in self-defeat

Eventually the energy returns
And you get the benefit that patience earns

If you scorn another for his way
You'll see yourself that way some day

You can let yourself believe
In the need to grieve
In order to relieve

To be still
With the beauty
Of being
Will keep you
Insightfully
Seeing

Sometimes it helps to go slow
So as to know
Which way to go

To be still in a public place
Can help you achieve a state of grace

On your suffering, to dwell and pause
Can allow you to discern a cause

Learning to let grievances go
Can give your mind something new to show

You can let yourself grieve
So you can learn to believe
Your sorrows, you can leave

The need to brood
Can be understood
If it furthers the good

To not despair
When life seems unfair
By retiring into your inward lair

It is a thought that's insane
That says you should never complain

To repeatedly endure
Can be a form of a cure
That will help relieve you when you feel unsure
To excessive agitation this will inure
And help keep your motives pure

Once you recover from your losses
You'll see what you learned from the process

If you mock for solidarity's sake
Just be aware your integrity is at stake

The world might not be as it may seem
Epistemological solipsism would mean it all is one's dream

Seeking power
Will make you dour
If, in doing so,
You sacrifice the flower

It will help you retire
From the need to conspire
If you'll limit your desire

You need not mind if people laugh
If you can stand the gaffe

It helps to follow where reason leads
So long as it produces virtuous deeds

The more you try to be nice
The more you'll do so without thinking twice

From anger you can set yourself free
By living your life compassionately

To have remorse
Over the use of force
Can set your life on a new course

To learn to be ok with being alone
Will help you get back to your inner home

To be willing to let yourself respond
Will help you stay out of the slough of despond

You can be self-respecting
Through frequent introspecting

When the devil makes his appearance
You can be happy if you've practiced virtue-adherence

To give a healthy measure of anagogic striving
Can give you a treasure of a heavenly deriving

If you're willing to concede
You'll have no need for greed

If humor does, you, discombobulate
It's time to look at the content of your slate

If you can handle rejection
You'll be more open to correction

The guidance of intuition is sometimes hard to discern
But from your mistakes is how, through your intuition, you can learn

It's okay to complain
If it helps you to reframe

Even if you have no skill
You still can have a good will

Use a soft voice
When you have a choice

Only from peace within
Can peace in the world begin

The key to contentment is to be serene
Even when others are mean

Try not to give another flack
Because you're likely to get it back

You can reform
Your need to perform
By learning to conform
To a new norm

A prerequisite for peace of mind
Is that your will be kind

If you practice virtue
No insult can hurt you

You'll make a serendipituous discovery
Once from loss you make a recovery

To see the error of one's ways
Will make for future better days

Sometimes to digress
Is to progress

Your life
Will be rife
With suffering
If you let anger
And thus languor
Destroy your buffering

If you live your life for the next thrill
Be careful not to sacrifice goodwill

The challenge is to avoid going rogue
Even when it has become the vogue

It's better to hold back
Than be quick to attack

Being a detractor
Of the malefactor
Can turn you into an over-reactor

Karma is a positive feedback loop
Decisions made today make for future decision's scoop

Trying to learn to not get psyched out
Will help you when experiencing self-doubt

When you're singled out for prejudice
Not angrily rebelling will help you handle this

It helps one not to fall into despair
If one knows one can self-repair

To see another change their ways
Never ceases to amaze

To keep your energy in balance
Can be one of your talents

It helps to learn to submit
When perseverating will not quit

If you can watch your appetite
You'll have a chance at gaining more insight

It's never too late to turn over a new leaf
It may cause pain but will end in pain's relief

You can abjure stealth
For the sake of mental health

If you choose too much to vaunt
Your guilty conscience will haunt

To live life with patience
Will help reduce temptations

Pondering gets you in touch with feeling
It calms your soul when you are reeling

When a joke causes pain
It's better to refrain

There is a virtue
There's no doubt
In learning not to shout

You can let it be your mission
To use your intuition
To describe the human condition

Men are often defined by how much they dare
Women are often defined by how much they care
Women can teach men to dare to care

If you've committed a mortal sin
Repentance can help you begin again

It's better to be meek
Even if you seem weak
Than another's harm to seek

To accept being an object of scorn
Will set you about being reborn

That the motives of others are inscrutable
Is a truth that's indisputable

It helps to confess
So as not to obsess

"It rains on the just and the unjust alike"
The key is not to let rain become spite

To be open to outside influence
Can turn influence into confluence
Just like working with industrious energy
Can turn energy into synergy

You can learn to inure
By learning to endure

Learning from a backward glance
Will help you put away the lance

A life that knows a solitude sublime
Will not need a rollicking good time

A higher desire
Seeks to retire
From worldly desire

When you live for a cause
You've no need for applause

You can learn from the process
Of trying not resent your losses

If you engage in too much reflection
You'll go into a state of dejection

Anger will only serve to do you in
It's better not to always try to win

If you can find a way to endure some strife
You will have a more fulfilling life

Once you get perspective
Life doesn't seem so defective

The nomothetic is all about the universal
But the idiographic can provide a reversal of the universal

You can make a decision
To sacrifice exacting precision
In order to grant remission

Accepting a degree of pain
Can help you stay sane

One can embark on the spiritual path to be pure
But its practical virtue is in helping you endure

If you're a person of virtue
No slight can hurt you

Whatever you do for fun
Keep compassion number one

Balance is best
Between activity and rest

The more you act in ways that are mean
The less likely you'll be serene

The soul will receive
What the mind will conceive
Based on what the intuition will perceive

The one who attacks
And whose morals are lax
Is at risk of getting into a wax

You can do what's right
By trying not to fight
So as not to lose sight
That it is not might
But insight
That makes right

Life is a process
Of learning from your losses

It's not the nature of the thing you choose
But your intention that renders you your dues

To be healthy
Try not to be stealthy

Dwelling with pure awareness
Can teach you fairness

The achievement of brilliance
Owes much to resilience

Mindfulness of your being
Is a way of seeing

Being kind
Will help you have
A sound mind

The soul that repents
And relents
Thereby possibly prevents
A chronic need for defense

It's better to be open and risk being susceptible
So, if needed, you'll be correctable

Reality may have designed
That you can find
Within your mind
The meaning of life defined

Ideally it would be great to be open all the time
But sometimes you need, your energy, to confine

Just because you die
Doesn't mean you won't get by

If you can stand the gaffe
You won't mind if others, at you, laugh

It can help you find a way out of despair
If you can find something for which to care

If you can find a way to endure hate
Your anger will usually abate

It's better to ignore
The peccadilloes you deplore
Rather than trying to even the score

Swearing an oath
Can impede personal growth

Anger can undo
The will to practice virtue

Cynicism
May be worthy of criticism
But too much criticism
Can result in cynicism

It can be due to jouissance when the elated
Becomes jaded

Familiarity breeds contempt on a daily basis
In times of crisis proximity brings homeostasis

Submission can be done for acquiescence
But civil disobedience also teaches lessons

Looking within your soul
Can help you self-console

The categorical imperative
Qualifies congruence as its declarative

There's nothing wrong in indulging in pleasure
So long as it's done in moderate measure

When you've done your best
You can put guilt to rest

Some people find their joy in causing others pain
For others, causing pain only causes themselves shame

If you act towards others in ways that are sarcastic
When others mock you, you may become bombastic

If you can settle for less
This attitude will self-bless

To let yourself be true
To the good in you
Can help you to construe
How to cultivate your own virtue

It can help contain
Your pain
By learning to refrain
From inveterately showing disdain

Learning to let things go
Can help prevent a row

If you, within the fracas, still can dwell
You'll have a chance at being well

If you don't mind being humble
This will help you bounce back from the bungle

When life seems unfair
You can repair
To your inward lair
And once you're there
You can take care
To find some things for which to share

Your conscience will direct your behavior
And can function as your own savior

To let thoughts arise of their own accord
Will help your sanity be restored

The more that you refrain from using stealth
The more this will redound to your mental health

Thoughts that induce anxiety
Are often based on contrariety

That soul is able to repent
That will let itself relent

It helps to have someone who will listen to us
And who will make an admission to us

It's normal to be, of some things, afraid
Sometimes it's better to be staid

There is nothing necessarily wrong with monkey mind
Because monkey mind can still be kind

Acting pretentious
May make you contentious

It would be great to tell everybody everything all the time
But you also need to self-confine

Going for the effect
Can make you self-reject

The idea of the dove
Seems like a picture of love

You'll lose touch
If you self-indulge too much

Communing with nature will help keep you calm
And put into your soul a healing balm

When someone tells you that you're awesome
The beauty within you will briefly blossom

If you express yourself in ways sardonic
This will be a brief but bitter tonic

When a thought's occasioned by a rhyme
You'll draw upon thoughts from a former time

Cyclical homeostasis is good
Sometimes to emote, other times to brood

If you want to find meaning in life
Be still in the midst of strife

Purity is evanescent
Virtue is incandescent
Joy is effervescent
These are found when in the present

To endure the smothers
Of others
Will help you forgive others
When you have your druthers

Intelligence is something to employ
In learning how to build and not destroy

In temperamental deadlock not to win
But ride out passion, then retreat within

You can have a mission
To explicate the human condition
So long as you practice submission
When you're in need of remission

To not worry if at times you flounder
Because you can always be a rebounder

The process of life is a dialectic
Remembering this helps when life gets hectic

Taking some time each day to deliberate and be still
Will help you develop goodwill

It helps to relocate your desire
When you notice you are starting to conspire

Inconveniences are inseparable from unfavorable judgment
This will teach you patience if you can bear it without begrudgement

Self-actualization depends
On a self that self-transcends

Part of doing what's right
Is to be polite

You can reframe
Pain
To let it wane

If it is your wont to act like a friend
You will be able, your friendships, to mend

Your life-expectancy will be short
If you react to every retort

It is indubitable
That evil is inscrutable

You can tell that two people are good friends
If they seek to further each others' ends

We get feedback from the environment
To let our worries go into retirement

You can be resigned
To what the public may, in you, find

You can have a propensity
For withstanding immensity

You need not always win
Because you can retreat within

It will help you be understanding
If you can be withstanding
When others have need for countermanding

When asked, speak the spontaneous truth
Or so would say the sayer of sooth

The key is to be open to receive
And be unwilling to deceive

Culture conditions, but if you are strange
You then can live within a different range

If you are young and smart
And you take to heart
That lying is an art
Be careful that you're integrity doesn't start
To come apart

The appraisal of an action should consult
The motive as much as the result

If you like to give others jeers
Watch out that you don't lose your peers

Self-restraint
Can make you a saint

Anagogic striving
Rules out conniving

If you can accept the blunder
This will help you not to thunder

Your character will have grown
When you accept that life is on loan

To find a way to tolerate remorse
Can set your life on a new course

To let the milieu, you, ensconce
And let your being make a response

If you feel compunction
You'll receive unction
Which will help you to function

A person with patience and understanding
Has no need to go about commanding

You can get to the other side
By riding out the ride

The divine dispensation
Decides which sensations to sanction

There's nothing wrong with being sociable
Being open and approachable

To accept
But not necessarily approve
Is a precept
That will behoove

To practice of obfuscation
Will cause self-agitation

If you like to prey on other people
May god have mercy on you when you're feeble

Learning to forgo resentment
Will help you have contentment

Learning to endure
Can be as good as a cure

Making a compassionate choice
Will help you find your beneficent voice

To be open to others influence
Can form a synergistic confluence

There's nothing wrong with wanting to share
If it keeps you out of despair

If you can find a way to endure hate
Patience can become a character trait

If you forsake kindness
You'll be prone to moral blindness

If you can learn to tolerate others
All will be your sisters and your brothers

Do people know about factory farms
And how their taste for meat maims and harms?

It is gut-wrenching to see an innocent make a bad move
Because the world will mercilessly reprove

When a concrete thought is agitating
Revert to second-order cogitating

To be open to all thoughts as much as you can
Will help you, others' attacks, to withstand

If you have no friends with which to converse
You can satisfy this need by writing verse

If you can learn to dwell alone in time
The life you lead will be a life sublime

If you can turn inward to find your joy
You will find meaning in meaning's employ

To believe in force
And the use of strength
Will make you feel worse
At length

Let worry be
To be worry free

In order to subsist
Survival will consist
In the ability to desist
From the will to willfully resist

If you will try to, your goodwill, retain
It will help if, from vice, you'll refrain

The next life's restitution
Will provide a faithful solution
To this life's destitution

To lengthen your attention span
Will help you understand
The idea of a divine plan

To be alone with the word
Will allow you to leave the herd

If you're diffident you doubt your powers
That's okay. You can still enjoy the flowers

It's okay to reiterate
So long as you're considerate

The key is not to be a countermander
Of those who would raise the dander

Being willing to be contrite
Will help you be polite

The goal is to be good
Even when you're misunderstood

To be endowed
With a personal cloud
Will keep you in a shroud
Buffered against the loud

By looking at the beauty of the trees up above
You will be living a life of sublime love

It will help you tolerate others
By being generous when you have your druthers

If you seek to astound
You will self-confound

The spiritual path may be embarked upon to be pure
But its practical virtue is in helping us endure

By repentance you are shriven
Through acts of atonement you are forgiven

If you judge a life based upon its results
You may miss whether reason, conscience, consults

That evil is inscrutable
Is indubitably indisputable
And indisputably indubitable

Endurance
Can bring assurance

You can be eccentric
And still be authentic

You can practice adherence
To the truth behind appearance

Mental health
Abjures stealth

To ease your anger with humility
Will help you act with civility

Human emotions are glad, sad and mad
Joy, fear and rage are the ways that they are had

A gentleman consults the feminine
Before he punishes with discipline

To be open to outside influence
Will help you live a life of congruence

If you can keep your temper cool
After you've acted like a fool
You can let love rule

Let virtue provide security
With a will aimed at purity

If you can find a way to endure hate
You'll find a way to self-congratulate

Though you may be rash at confiding things
You can go neurotic hiding things

People have a right to speak their mind
It's up to you to if this makes you unkind

You do not have to comply
With others who tell you to lie

We all have energy
To form a synergy
To channel our influence
Into a confluence
All to be set free in a shared sense of congruence

Honesty
Is the best way to be
The virtuous commend you
When in you, this, they see

In well-being, material goods can play a role
So long as we don't lose the well-being of our soul

It helps to have commiserated
With those who have been eviscerated

When someone is corrupt they may love it
Yet their fate before God, no one would covet

You'll be ok on the day you die
If you did not subordinate the truth to the lie

Homeostasis has been achieved
Once you've gotten over that over which you grieved

Your emotions approximate perfection
When they don't depend upon an in-person connection

We all have a right to respect
It is what we all would expect
But sometimes when you get a slight
You have to forgo this right
In order, with others, to reconnect

If you are a person who's skillful
Let's hope you won't use it in ways too willful

Just because you breathe your last on your dying day
Does not mean that consciousness goes away

A brick-layer
Can still be a soothsayer

To know you can pick yourself up after you fall
Can help ease the gall

You can endure a bit of humiliation
For the sake of conciliation

You're in sorrow
When you feel you have nothing to borrow
From tomorrow

When in sorrow you resume
To shower the bloom
The cure for your ills
Will be blossoming soon

God seems brilliant
When the humanities and the sciences are consilient

To routinely lie to get your way
Is to give your soul away

Fear of becoming that which you are loath to be
Can teach humility

To fall back on a habitual routine
Can help when life is mean

It is an insight
To learn that it can be right
Not to fight

It is a lesson
That confession
Can lessen
Obsession

A thought that passes through the intellect
Experience can later resurrect

To find a way to contract and condense
Is to find a way to let healing commence

It is an error
That, in trying to make life fairer
You invoke the use of terror

If you harp on something too much
With reality, you may lose touch

You'll be able to relent
If you're willing to repent

If you over-indulge in the sensual
You're breakdown will be eventual

In coping with what seems real
It helps to not conceal
How you feel

You can remedy your loss
By letting go of the opportunity cost

You can pay forward the generosity of others
By being generous when you have your druthers

To decompensate, through impulsiveness, from being whole
Is to not be thinking of your long-term goal

That person is wise
Who complies
With a willingness to compromise

To go pell-mell for pleasure
Will rob you of sublimation's treasure

We count as a virtue
What temperance lets accrue

If you seek to deceive
You'll have reason to grieve

Immoderate gratification of desire
Can leave you in a quagmire

A healing thought is conditional
Upon it being original
And upon it being, of compassion, provisional

Words take on meanings
Of their user's leanings

Sometimes it's better to be tame and self-restrain
To not lose more than you would gain

To transcend yourself
Is to dispose of stealth

Genius is a happy accident
That redounds to its glory in thoughts subsequent

To read to contract
To write to condense
Though not a method exact
It helps to get you hence

When you start to obsess
It's time, your goal, to reassess

Clichés can be wise
In what they advise

Eloquence
Has a redolence
Of benevolence

It helps to talk about pain
In order to re-frame

To not want to use rage
To get passed a stage
But rather get passed the stage
Of using rage

A need for glory
Can rankle your story

If you act with ire
Be careful not to "fan the flames of your imagination on fire." --Abraham A. Low

Sometimes it's better to not think but just to feel
To let yourself heal

If you live in the eternal now
You don't seek to cow
But to allow

To introspect
Is to self-inspect

The challenge is to not become bombastic
When someone is sarcastic

To overcome greed
Will you help someone in need

The best thing is to not just be strong
But to be willing to admit it when you are wrong

Objectives in this world may have a role
But true meaning comes from within the soul

To be flexible
Is to be correctible

It is possible to come to be at home
With being alone

A benefit of being staid
Is that you can brace yourself when you're afraid

In solitude in your seclusion
You can process a delusion

The truth can set you free
To live authentically

A person who is genuine
Can forgo a dominion

To have a cooperative attitude
Can foster gratitude

All will solace
Each other's sorrow
In the polis
Of tomorrow

Attending to your soul
Can be part of the goal
Of keeping the collective whole

Using deception
Can be the inception
Of a misconception
Of the need to use deception

That which is surreal
May be a reflection of how you feel

When the time comes to retreat within
An interior life then can begin

When you get too caught up in the need for power
It's time to go back to honoring the flower

You can create a cocoon of envelopment
Through inner development

It's not how much you push and shove
But how much you love

If you go all out to be superior
You may have motives ulterior

You may find
That the mind
Can be defined
As designed
To be resigned
In order to be kind

The good in truth
Is characterized by ruth

When perfidy does betray
It's better to go your own way
Than have insults to say

Learning to endure
For the sake of being pure
Will help you feel secure

You'll be able to withstand the attack
The less you give it back

Letting the energy simmer down
Can turn your fate back around

Women condition men to be polite
By showing them the folly of the need to fight

At the uttermost end of pain
Life can begin again

Spirituality does not seek gain
But consists in accepting pain

If you're wise you know what you won't do
And you know what you will seek to see through

Priding yourself
On your skill
Can lead to ill-will
Confiding in yourself
While holding still
Can generate goodwill

Forswearing the life of the senses
Is where spirituality commences

If you don't mind being alone
You can call many places your home

Spirituality teaches your consciousness
How to withstand remonstrances

To tell yourself when to say when
Is to return your soul to grace again

The key is to let people have their fun
And still keep compassion number one

The more you can withstand
The less you'll need to make a demand

Inertia may feel like it's pushing you towards death
But it's all love when you catch your breath

To not be derisive
Towards the indecisive

If can be your forte
To not need to retort

Although your life may be tumultuous
Your life's nature can still be congruous
And since that's the case
Happiness can take place

If you complain
And do so
With tact
You'll refrain
From needing
To exact

To be free of deceit can save your soul
Being free of deceit can be your overriding goal

To console
Is to join with another's soul

You may want to, your conscience, consult
Before going for the result

The preconscious mind can give you a gift
To heal a moment's momentary rift

If you forgo anger you can be less demeaning
This can be how you make meaning

To be within a cloud
In a public place
Can provide a shroud
That occasions grace

Through corruption you may make a short-term gain
But you'll lose your integrity if, from corruption, you can't refrain

What the law can't enforce
Virtue will reconcile in due course

Compassion is worth more than gold
Patience helps it to unfold

Eventually the energy will settle
And bring you back into fine fettle

You can write for the sake of discovery
Because it brings recovery

What it the nature of élan vital?
It's beyond the nature of the mortal

If through kindness you've overcome your fear of judgment after death
You'll be less afraid as you draw your last breath

Contemplation can help you feel strong
When you feel you don't belong

If you habitually use deceit to frequently get your way
In the end you'll have given your only soul away

When your worldly hope has gone away
You can base your hope on heaven's day

Making a confession
Can ease depression

Nice people in this world are a blessing
They give you reason to keep confessing

You will find relief
Once you've processed grief

In this world you may feel like a pariah
But so was many a messiah

Although you may not have children of your own
You can make the world a better place for children to call home

The world checks you
Regeneration perfects you

To go into the cloud of unknowing
Will help you to be anger-forgoing

Getting through depression
Can teach you a lesson

Abstinence enthuses grace
And lets virtue take place

You'll be able to suffer ignominy
If you treat others with bonhomie

You can retire
From the desire
To conspire

You can share
About what you care
To emerge from despair

It can be one of your joys
To be the virtue that virtue employs

You can refrain
From casting blame
To let the pain
Wane

If you let yourself be habitually aggressive
Your direction will be regressive

Patience is the key
To becoming who you want to be

You can learn to use the retort
Only as a last resort

To be in the flow
Is to let things go

You can give your thoughts some room
To let beauty bloom

You don't need to be clever
So long as you are willing to endeavor

You can forgo righteous indignation
For the sake of virtue-integration

It's hard at times to know if opposition is real
Or if it is a function of how, at the time, you feel

When you self-immure
Your worries can find a cure

You can let your thoughts simmer down
Until stability comes back around

Once you weather the storm
Your creativity is reborn

You can make a retreat
From the use of deceit

Trees
Provide love
From above

It's better not deride for solidarity's sake
Because it's your integrity that is at stake

An introspective interior life
Can ease internal strife

The soul has unction
When anointed by compunction

Let stillness instill
The birth of goodwill

Poignant tears
Transcend fears

When a thought rings true
It resonates with you

If you're willing to make a concession
You'll be able to make a confession

To let your heart open
It helps to be soft-spoken

When you can let down your defenses
Recovery commences

Consciousness is all that does abide
You'll keep it pure if you learn to self-confide

To go into a cocoon
To let your inner beauty bloom

Learning to accept changes
Will help when life estranges

You can develop a propensity
For withstanding immensity

If you can learn to endure the insult
A life of virtue will be the result

It is understood
That taking time to brood
Could further the greater good

You can welcome everything in
So you can have a clean slate again

You'll be alright
If you decline to set right
Every little slight

Endurance gives you stamina
To honor the anima

Over time anger will attenuate
The more you sublimate

Taking time to brood
Can put you in a better mood

The allure
Of the pure
Can make you chaste
Teaching moderation
Of soul-sensation
Upon which virtue's based

Ethics, morality and virtue
Are of love compact when true

If you're feeble
You can draw hope from the steeple

The angels may talk through you
And teach you what to construe

If you don't mind being seen
Your conscience can be clean

If you offer charity right now
An auspicious future your perception will endow

The way of the saint
Is to work so hard you might faint
And still in the face of adversity have restraint

Accepting a stimulating tenseness
Will help you lower your defenses

Letting go of conditions of worth
Can give your spirit a rebirth

By taking time to reflect
You become aware of what you introject

Giving free reign to anger will only do you in
Each time you do so, the more you'll do it again

Using force
As a recourse
Will bring remorse
In due course

The intangibles that transcend this earthly realm
Will give you guidance when you're at the helm

If you stake your peace on the external
You're overlooking the eternal

If you want to be a force for good
You'll not mind if you're a bit misunderstood

The is/ought divide
Is what you cross when you confide

When you're inspired
Love has transpired

Listening to your muse
Takes away your blues

It's better to let go of that thought
That in resentment gets you caught

Creative thoughts develop
After they envelop

Needing to compete
Always ends in self-defeat

The utilitarian calculus should only be undertaken in determining whether to sacrifice an interest of oneself
Never to sacrifice an interest of someone else

Full-lotus posture
Helps you
To refine
And distill
Unto a love
Divine

When you realize you're doing all that you need to do
The world will take on a different hue

The conclusion of this life cannot sever
Universal truth gained through endeavor
For once learned, the Eternal Verities stay with us forever

The more you can lower your defenses
The less need you'll have for pretenses

To be open to possibility
Can give you a compassionate ability

A human connection
Is like a confection
If it fosters
Salubrious reflection

Life is a work-in-progress
In which you learn from your losses
As all part of the process

When competition is superseded by cooperation
You can enjoy a compassionate mode of operation

The interior life rests enveloped in insulation
Dwelling within which provides consolation

Two perplexing questions are:
"How much is personal to me
And how much can everyone else see?"
And:
"How much is personal to you
And how much can everyone else view?"

If you laugh at someone else's pain
Just remember one day you will feel shame
When someone laughs at you in ways the same

What's more important than wealth
Is transcending yourself

You can learn to let go
To let your feelings show

There's no punishment that's so condign
That nature can't resolve in time

Benevolence
Always has relevance

The mind
Has many modes
From travelling
Down many roads

Taking time to look within
Can help you begin
Your life over again

The individual soul
Is part of a larger whole

To reflect pensively
Is to think non-defensively

If you can try to withstand it when someone gives you a shove
Synergy will turn this energy into love

Eventually the energy settles down
And then your peace of mind can come back around

You become weary
Of theory
When you have analysis
Paralysis

The source of the illustrious
Resides in the industrious

Angels have talents
For keeping people in balance

Drifting in space
Can cure the ills of haste

To speak in parole
And write in langue
Is to energize the soul
And calm it with a song

Credulity
By definition
Sparks joy
Upon recognition

Overindulgence in feeling
Can set you reeling

To not judge someone by the standards of society
But by how you feel their anxiety

Things come back into focus
After you internalize your locus

The key to not let life estrange you
Is when someone disdains you
To still let virtue restrain you

Clichés
May no longer amaze
But they can still get you through the phase
Of when you are in a malaise

Language is an amazing thing
It lets sorrow take wing

Confession plays a role
In nurturing the soul

The balm
Will give you a buffer
And keep you calm
When you suffer

You'll never go out of style
So long as you live for a cause that's worthwhile

Some people obey the law
Because they must
Other people obey the law
Because in higher laws they trust

Learning from the ethereal
To transcend the self
Is worth more than material
Wealth

You can keep things in perspective
By staying introspective

When someone is humorously histrionic
It heals like a tonic

When you make a self-disclosure
That results in self-exposure
Although it may not have been kosher
It can ultimately bring about cloture

Eventually impulses convert into locutions
Bringing creative solutions

If you engage in thoughtful deliberation
You'll show others thoughtful consideration

The virtue of patience
Is one of spirituality's creations

In heaven we will see what other people think
And give each other for our faults a wink

To validate what a person is feeling
Means you've set them on their way to healing

A wish to be effective
At deception
Is a wish that is defective
At its inception

You'll be fine even if you don't fit in
Because in solitude you can begin again

Each place has its own spirit of vibe
It's a phenomenon that's hard to describe

Going into public and holding still
To let your being fill
Will help you maintain goodwill

Tumult
In the crucible
Provides a result
That is usable

Offering someone reassurance
Will help give them endurance

Even though you may feel shame
You are not necessarily to blame

It's hard to refrain
From importunity when in pain

To let yourself get lost in thought
Can help you recover the homeostasis you sought

To restrain the appetite
For the sake of insight

Universal truths are delectable
So long as they're correctible

Accepting your brethren in this story
Will in heaven redound to your glory

Senescence
Is a return to innocence

Universal morality
Is based on a plurality
Of diverse forms of cultural reality

Congruence will bless
If you don't feel you need to repress
The willingness to second-guess

To withstand hate
Without needing to execrate
Can make you great

When evil ones attack
But are within the law
The need to give it back
Can be a fatal flaw

A true friend
Has a will to commend

Taking time to self-immure
Can help you find a cure
When life leaves you feeling unsure

To be long-suffering
And practice forbearance
Can give you a buffering
For the sake of coherence

To concede
The need
For self-confession
Is to move away
From the ways
Of aggression

To forgo this world's pleasure
And, through anagogic striving,
Obtain the afterlife's treasure
Of a heavenly deriving

To have a preference
For deference
As a point of reference

It's a miracle
To live inside the spherical
By being spiritual

You can overcome your grief
By turning over a new leaf

To refrain
From assigning blame
When you don't know
From where the fault came

A person without need to feel superior
Will not have motives ulterior

A cooperative attitude
Can foster gratitude
By giving others latitude

The morality
Of the norms
Comes in a plurality
Of different forms

To immerse yourself in the ocean's undulations
Can provide you with spiritual sensations

Turning over a new leaf
Can provide a belief
That will provide relief
From grief

Phrases that are sententious
Will not be pretentious
So long as they are conscientious

To be a saint
Is not to be without taint
But to have self-restraint
When met with complaint

Acceptance that we are ultimately alone
Can be a helpful gnome

The goal is to be happy in the afterlife
For this philosophy can be a midwife

If you regularly achieve transcendence
This will benefit your descendants

Transcending limitation
Produces inspiration

If we all took some time to be seclusive
This practice would be conducive
To a society that's inclusive

Trials and tribulation
Can result in character-creation

When someone
With their energy
Gives you a shove
You can form a synergy
To turn this energy
Into love

It's better not to lie
In the afterlife we'll know why

There's a heavenly logic
To the anagogic

You can take a degree of pain
In order to stay sane

Lying to be efficacious
Will make you mendacious
And ultimately will make you umbrageous

You can engage in introspection
To become aware of introjection
For the sake of redirection

Overemphasis on propriety
Can cause undue anxiety

When you feel salubrious
You've resolved feeling dubious

If you can retire into the self
You won't need material wealth

You transcend
When you give a hand to lend

You can take time for reflection
For the sake of detection
Of the unconscious introjection

Your constitution will eventually soften
By taking time to contemplate often

It's ok to believe
In the need to grieve
To your sorrow relieve

Maintaining a degree of independence
Will help you achieve transcendence
From co-dependence

There's no need for skills proficient
The soul is self-sufficient

You can bring your backstage to the fore
So you will not keep secrets any more

Giving others latitude
Will foster gratitude

Not needing to keep hope
Obsessively in scope
Will help you cope

It is good to beat a hasty retreat
At the intention to use deceit

A virtuous non-conformist
Can be a moral reformist

Your life will become dour
If you forsake the flower
For the sake of worldly power

By repentance your misdeeds are forgiven
Through penitence you are atoned and thereby shriven

Candor
And sincerity
Subordinates grandeur
To charity

Contemplation taken to arrive at hope
Can be a mechanism by which you cope

Rather than casting an insult
First your conscience consult
So as to accept the result

You'll learn from a mistake
Once you realize all that is at stake

When you suffer
You gain a buffer
That helps you when you suffer

Seeking an even-tempered calm
Will turn your soul into balm

True love is, when after passion subsides,
A lasting friendship abides

Humility is what it takes
To learn from your mistakes

Intuition navigates what's existentially real
Based on how you personally feel

You can tell a person's explanatory style
Based on that at which they smile

Having the patience to wait
Will help you accept your fate

Processing remorse
Can put your life on a new course

To abide with suffering
As it comes and goes
Provides a buffering
That grows

You can overcome gloom
If you give reflection room

When you cease to conspire
New life can then transpire

If you learn to inure
This will help you feel secure

If you seek to understand
You'll have no need to reprimand

The individual soul
Plays a role
In keeping the collective whole

You won't have motives ulterior
If you have a life interior

To mental health it can be conducive
If you are periodically reclusive

You'll find hope
When at the end of your rope
If you've used congruence to cope

If you can endure perseveration
Over its duration
You can recover a state of elation

When a person lies
Myopia, this implies

Once you're resigned
To the subtlety of your speech
Peace of mind
Comes within reach

Your suffering will eventually be replete
If you mendaciously use deceit

The willingness to call a truce
Of peace of mind does this conduce

The more your attachments decrease
The more you'll attain to peace

Musing on mindfulness generates insight
By bringing the unconscious to light

The categorical imperative
Is based on the declarative
Of the virtue of the comparative

Sometimes when you're in despair
It helps to find something to share

It helps to jettison a thought
When in inertia you get caught

After you take time to look within
A new chapter can begin

Once you've recorded the gestalt
Things seem less your fault

What you view internally
Is there eternally

Though some thoughts may be trite
They still can have insight
To help you do what's right

You can let your body condense
To let healing commence

With your higher power you can have a connection
Through frequent introspection

It can help your soul heal
When you share how you feel

The practice of toleration
Can give your sorrows migration

If you feel you have something to prove
Moderation does behoove

Observing a paradox
Can help you think outside the box

You recover once you integrate
That over which you perseverate

Learning to manage your spirit
Will help you not to fear it

When others' situations you habitually seek to understand
You be less inclined to use the reprimand

If you make an obdurate refusal
To accept an untoward fate
Giving a book a perusal
Can return you to a peaceful state

If you feel that you are becoming mean
It helps to find something for which to come clean

The categorical imperative tells us what to do
The utilitarian calculus tells us what good to construe

The utilitarian model of transcendent expedience
Transcends unquestioning obedience

Keeping the collective whole
Is one of education's goal

Energy can provide impetus
When it departs from the sensuous

There is such a thing as good intention
But it's the motive that's more worth mention

You can always go within
When you cannot win

What your thought consecrates
Your soul emanates

Philosophic speculation is a palliative
When life seems too hard to live

Just because you take umbrage doesn't mean you resent
You may just take shade to let your thoughts relent

Sublimation provides enthusiasm
To cross a momentary chasm

You cannot condemn a person for their wrath
If you've never traveled down their path

Its' never too late
To transcend your fate

Sometimes it helps to go deep inside
When you need to ride out agitation's ride

It helps to heal remorse
By letting time take its course

When you show a person disdain
You're not considering their pain

After a while studied thoughts arise spontaneously
And are used extemporaneously

If you fail at going to an extreme
It's time to go back to observing the golden mean

It's folly for a person to think they are better than other people
Because one day they too will be feeble

Propinquity allows the space
For friendship to take place

Your will affects
What the collective will effects

Drifting in space
Let's creativity take place

Changing your attitude
In the direction of cultivating gratitude
Will help you give latitude

It's nice to be ensconced in your own little world
To let your being become unfurled

It helps to let energy distill
By holding still

If you regularly engage in reflection
This will help you handle rejection

Your interior life will be your salvation
Once the world ceases to give you salutation

Socratic irony bestowed
Many a philosophic road

You can say nope
To dope
By loving hugs
More than drugs

Virtue makes a retreat
At the temptation to use deceit

Deliberation
Brings liberation

If you have a need to be a saint
Neglecting your being to the point you'd faint
And see in this the means to supersede the mortal taint
Just remember that it is your being
That sets the lens through which your eyes are seeing

Life is a
Lesson in
Living with
Loss without
Losing the
Longing to
Love

www.ingramcontent.com/pod-product-compliance
Lightning Source LLC
Chambersburg PA
CBHW081633040426
42449CB00014B/3296